CONTEMPORARY WOOD ENGRAVERS
Series Editor: Simon Brett

CONTEMPORARY WOOD ENGRAVERS is a new series of monographs profiling those who make up the lively state of wood engraving, whether they work as printmakers, illustrators or in the production of fine books. The series begins with artists from Britain and the United States; others from elsewhere in the world will be introduced in due course to give an international view. It will also include occasional studies of artists of the recent past whose work has been insufficiently appreciated or deserves reassessment in the light of contemporary practice. The books in the series are designed to appeal not only to the specialist but also to anyone interested in the visual arts.

GEOFFREY WALES made prints which were a central part of the British response to modernism and used wood engraving, at the time of its lowest ebb, to do so. He was one of very few artists who have taken the medium from illustration all the way into abstraction - the shoreline of Norfolk and of his native Kent remaining an inspiration for the whole length of the journey. The glimmer and beauty of the sea inspired him all his life. Wales had successes in the private press movement of the 'thirties and through the 'fifties, but his later, more adventurous work was scarcely seen, let alone appreciated, in his lifetime. Hilary Chapman's pioneering study places his work in the context of the advanced printmaking of its time and pays tribute to an artist of quiet but revolutionary integrity - our unrecognised contemporary.

HILARY CHAPMAN, M.A. is a freelance art historian who writes and lectures on prints. She also has a gallery in London which specialises in British prints of the early twentieth century.

Geoffrey Wales

❧ CONTEMPORARY WOOD ENGRAVERS ❧
SERIES EDITOR: SIMON BRETT

Geoffrey Wales

by

Hilary Chapman

Primrose Hill Press
Oak Knoll Press

© copyright Hilary Chapman 1998
© Illustrations copyright Geoffrey Wales Estate 1998

No part of this book may be reproduced in any form or by any means
without the prior permission in writing from the publisher.

ISBN: 1 90164 803 6
Primrose Hill Press

ISBN: 1 884718 55 8
Oak Knoll Press

British Library Cataloguing-in-Publication Data.
A catalogue record for this book is available from The British Library.

Contemporary Wood Engravers
Series Editor: Simon Brett
No. 1

Published in 1998 by
Primrose Hill Press Ltd
58 Carey Street, London WC2A 2JB
United Kingdom
and
Oak Knoll Press
414 Delaware Street, New Castle, DE 19720
USA

Printed in Great Britain by
Hobbs the Printers, Southampton

ACKNOWLEDGEMENTS

My thanks go to the artist's widow, Marjorie Wales, whose wish to see her husband's artistic achievements properly recognised resulted in a memorial exhibition of his work in London in 1991 and spurred the production of this book. I would like to thank also their daughters, Elizabeth and Philomine, for their helpful insights into their father's personality and work; John Riches for information on Geoffrey's period of teaching in Norwich; John O'Connor for information on the Royal College of Art in the 1930s; and Ruth Barker and Peter Baldwin for facts and anecdotes on the Reverend Willis Feast and the Norwich 20 Group. My thanks also go to Simon Brett for thoughtful and encouraging editing, and to Marjorie Allthorpe-Guyton who first introduced me to the remarkable wood engravings of Geoffrey Wales.

Hilary Chapman 1998

CONTENTS

LIST OF ILLUSTRATIONS IN THE TEXT

Cover
Water Garden. 1967/68. 167x280mm

Frontispiece
Photograph of Geoffrey Wales, c. 1965

Illustrations in text

THE WOOD ENGRAVINGS

About two-thirds of the wood engravings are reproduced actual size. Of the remaining third, some have had to be reduced by as much as 50%, lessening their impact considerably, especially in relation to those which are seen full size. Reduction is indicated in the captions opposite plates 1-45, between pages 27 and 117.

GEOFFREY WALES occupies a unique place in the history of wood engraving. At the time of the medium's lowest ebb and undeterred by lack of interest, he made wood engravings which are an authentic part of the British response to modernism. They demonstrate a progression from the decorative and illustrative, through the neo-romantic and semi-cubist, to works of almost pure abstraction. Probably no other artist in the medium has explored so fully, so minutely, and yet so privately, the full potential of the twentieth century aesthetic.

Geoffrey Wales was a Kentish man, born on the 26th May 1912 in Margate and brought up in the Westbrook area of the town. His grandfather had owned one of the largest building firms in Thanet and his father, Ernest, was employed in the family business. Ernest married a local girl, Kathleen, who had three sons, Geoffrey being the eldest. Geoffrey enjoyed the surroundings of that seaside town and showed an early ability for drawing and painting the marine subject matter with which he was familiar. Whilst at Thanet School of Art from 1929-33, he distinguished himself as a fine draughtsman and watercolourist and demonstrated a particular talent for graphic design. His early style indicated an empathy with the strong colour and flattened, simplified forms of modernism which typified the decorative design of the period, and in 1932 he won a competition to design a playing card for Messrs. de la Rue (Fig. 1). The award of £250 enabled him to study at the Royal College of Art in London. Geoffrey Wales arrived at the Royal College in 1933 and began as a student in the School of Design. At this time, many talented and progressive artists were taking up teaching appointments at the College, creating an exciting atmosphere. During the 1930s the staff at the School of Design included Barnett Freedman, Edward Bawden, John Nash, Paul Nash and Eric Ravilious. Such artists had all been students at the College during the previous decade and were now considered to be at the forefront of modern art in Britain.[1]

---

[1] Frayling, Christopher, *The Royal College of Art*, London 1967, p.100ff.

1

Figure 1
Summer Holidays,
design in colour for a playing
card for de la Rue, 1932,
80x50mm

Wood engraving was strongly promoted, due no doubt to the influence of the Nashes and Ravilious; and Geoffrey Wales studied the craft under the tutorship of John Nash and Bawden. He also studied in the School of Engraving under Robert Austin and Malcolm Osborne, and, at the end of his three years, he held Diplomas in Design, in Lithography and in Wood Engraving.

The precision, the concentration and the clarity of thought necessary to produce wood engravings appealed to his sharp intellect and reflective nature and caused him to adopt the woodblock as his preferred matrix for printmaking. He was undoubtedly influenced by the tutors at the College, as many of the compositions of his earlier wood engravings show similarities in style - to those of Eric Ravilious in particular. He also admired the severity of line in Paul Nash's engravings and sought to emulate it. But Geoffrey Wales was no imitator, and even these early wood engravings display an originality in their design and execution which indicate an artist of individuality and imagination. His sensitivity to spatial arrangement and pictorial composition is evidenced in a typical, small scale work of the period called Waterfall (Fig. 2). A certain controlled formality and precision in the engraving of this print is relieved by the movement and rhythm in the tree shapes and the splashing water. Even from an early stage

2

Figure 2: **Waterfall**, wood engraving, 1936, 50x125mm

in his work, he was able to resolve the tension between the hard edged linearity and the glyptic vitality of wood engraving, a vitality which relies fundamentally on the energy behind the cut marks.

Although printmaking was to be Geoffrey Wales' chosen field, painting was not neglected, especially mural painting. In 1936 he helped Barnett Freedman with his commission for the decoration of the Strand Underpass for the Coronation of George VI and Queen Elizabeth. This was a large, colourful mural with a nautical theme, including sailing ships and mermaids: highly pleasing material for him (Fig. 3). He also assisted John Nash in his decorations for the British Pavilion at the 1937 Paris Exhibition. John and Christine Nash were to become great friends and he was often invited to stay at their cottage in Buckinghamshire. He enjoyed their company and hospitality but was less happy on the occasions when they insisted he join in with their country dancing in the garden! Other friends and contemporaries at the Royal College were Frank Martin, Norman Janes and John O'Connor, an artist who also demonstrated an early predilection for wood engraving under the influence of Eric Ravilious and later developed his own highly individual approach as a painter and illustrator. Most importantly, at the Royal College Geoffrey had met his future wife, Marjorie Skeeles, a student in the School of Design who left after gaining her diploma to take up a teaching appointment with the Canterbury Art Schools.

Geoffrey was awarded a fourth year at the College in acknowledgement of his achievements in the Schools of Design and Engraving. In July 1937, he took a short course on Typography at the Central School, and then took up a teaching job which entailed

3

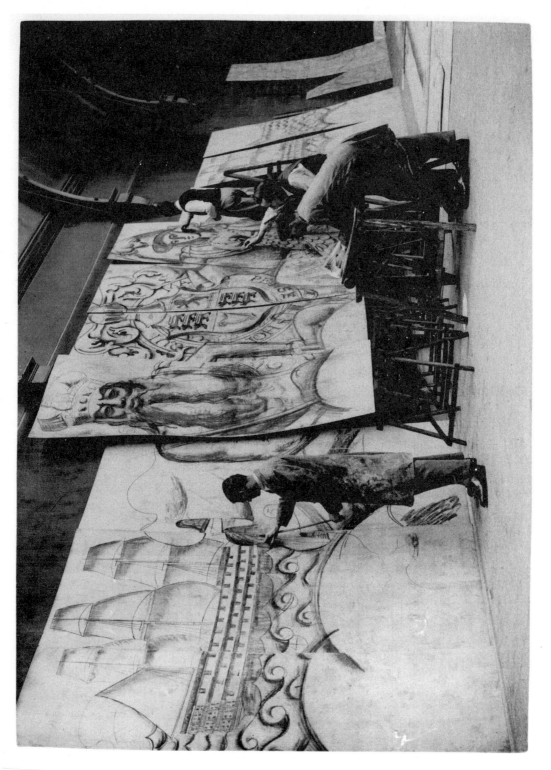

Figure 3: Geoffrey Wales (left) with Barnett Freedman and two other students working on a mural for the Strand Underpass, 1936 (Photograph: the artist's family)

4

travelling between Folkestone, Thanet and Canterbury Schools of Art. At Thanet, he was to be instrumental in the development of one student in particular: Monica Poole attended his class on book illustration and was recommended to try wood engraving. Geoffrey introduced her to the craft, sent her to T.E. Lawrence for the tools and equipment and encouraged her to begin her distinguished career as a wood engraver.

At Canterbury, Geoffrey met up again with Marjorie Skeeles. Friendship developed into courtship and engagement. But it was now 1940, and, as the Second World War took a further dangerous step, the art schools in Kent were closed and the teachers became eligible for call-up. Geoffrey and Marjorie obtained a Special Licence and were married on the 1st of August; on the 11th Geoffrey received his call-up papers for the Royal Air Force. The couple suffered a long, enforced separation from 1943 to 1946, when Geoffrey was away with his

Figure 4: Title Page for *The Pilgrim Fathers*, Golden Cockerel Press, 1939, wood engraving, 50x50mm

squadron in Corsica and Italy. During this time he spent a period in hospital in Palestine, recovering from jaundice. He wrote poems, which he sent back to Marjorie, and, like so many other servicemen, managed to find an inner strength to reconcile himself to the war. He was demobbed as a Flight Lieutenant.

After the war, he returned to Kent and to teaching. That was a career to which he would bring remarkable qualities of care and dedication, but which would never obscure his art.

" Weather Permitting "
. . . *A Masque of the Seasons*

PRESENTED BY THE STUDENTS

CHRISTMAS DANCE

PROGRAMME

WEDNESDAY, 21st DECEMBER, 1938

THANET SCHOOL OF ART

Figure 5: Cover for the programme to the Thanet School of Art Christmas Dance, 1938, wood engraving, 70x110mm

During his last year at the Royal College, Geoffrey Wales had shown his abilities as an illustrator, and had been commissioned by the Golden Cockerel Press to produce illustrations for an edition of *The Pilgrim Fathers*, which was published in 1939. The eight illustrations were executed in a broad style, the vigorous compositions complementing the story of that arduous adventure - especially on the title page for which he designed a small but animated scene of a ship on storm-tossed sea (Fig. 4). The book greatly pleased the Director of the Golden Cockerel Press, Christopher Sandford:

> Shall we then escape a charge of immodesty when we claim that *The Pilgrim Fathers* is one of the nicest books we have ever made - agreeable in its proportions, tasteful binding, beautiful paper, elegant typography and exceptionally pleasant and dexterous engravings, all harmonising with the charming content.[2]

The early wood engravings of Geoffrey Wales were indeed 'pleasant and dexterous', having an undoubtedly decorative quality and, now, a period charm. Colour was often employed using lino blocks; the combination of yellow and blue predominated and enhanced the nautical flavour of such prints as Yellow Tower (Pl. 2). The use of colour in wood engraving was something he was to discard in later work, however, and to discourage in his pupils. He urged the printmaker to discover the colour that lay within the black and white. Many of the works produced in the late 1930s and early 1940s were commissioned as illustrations or as advertising by commercial firms and were rarely editioned as individual prints. There are, however, two unusual wood engravings entitled Northern Waters and Sharp Attack (Pl. 3), which were produced during the war years and which, in their angry, jagged forms, reflect Geoffrey's responses and experiences. The vigorous and more expressionistic style of these prints, with their complex content, indicate a first move away from the more restrained and decorative style he had initially adopted.

Geoffrey Wales' wood engravings were mostly executed as part of a private and personal creativity. However, in the early days, he was more than happy to fulfil the commissions for prints that came his way: illustrations for commercial magazines and periodicals such as *Punch* and *Homes and Gardens,* and colourful advertisements for firms such as Morton Sundour Fabrics Ltd., of Carlisle. He even provided decorations for programmes, cards and invitations for Art Societies

---

[2] Chambers, David and Sandford, Christopher, *Pertelote*, Part II from the Bibliography of the Golden Cockerel Press, 1939-1943, Private Libraries Association, 1943, p.37.

Figure 6: **Spring Morning,** wood engraving, 1948, 172x124mm

and groups in the Folkestone area, of which he was a member (Fig. 5). His serious work was exhibited regularly, at the Society of Wood Engravers, of which he was invited to become a member in 1946, and with the Royal Society of Painter-Etchers and Engravers from 1948. It was admired by other wood engravers and several examples were acquired by John Buckland Wright. Margaret Pilkington, the long-serving secretary of the Society of Wood Engravers, purchased two, Quiet Afternoon and Bright Morning (Pl. 13), the latter passing into the extensive collection of wood engravings that she formed for the Whitworth Art Gallery in Manchester.[3]

Some of Geoffrey's prints of the late 1940s show an uncharacteristic interest in the figure, and had an undeniably romantic element, introducing a flowing, sensuous line into his formal repertoire (Fig. 6). The content of these engravings may represent rebirth and renewal after the hardships, deprivations and separations of the war. This new subject matter appeared around 1947, when stability and security had returned into Geoffrey's life. He was then re-settled with Marjorie and his two young daughters in a cottage which stood in the grounds of Marjorie's parents' home at Lyminge. Here he began a steady production of independent wood engravings and began to keep an edition book where meticulous records of each print, its edition number, and details of any sales or related exhibitions were entered. Wood engraving was an absorbing, self-contained occupation for him, which had the added advantage of being carried out in a small space and with the minimum of equipment. He never used a press, but printed each impression by hand, using an agate burnisher or the back of a spoon. He engraved and printed at a small table in a room in the family home. He was happy to work within the family environment that he valued greatly, but he struggled to find the time and energy for his printmaking after the demands of his peripatetic teaching (during day and evening), and his young family.

Geoffrey had more commissions for illustrations during the 1950s, for the Kynoch Press, the Golden Cockerel Press and the Folio Society. He produced imaginative and pictorially exciting images for these publications; some of which hinted at further newly evolving styles.

The *Kynoch Diary* for 1950 contains an illustration for every month, each design a successful combination of decoration, textural effect and some aspect of a new compositional form, while in the small cartouches

---

[3] Catalogue to Exhibition at Whitworth Art Gallery, Manchester, 26 Jan - 1 June 1991, Margaret Pilkington, 1891-1974.

Figure 7: Frontispiece to *Nelson's Letters from the Leeward Islands*, Golden Cockerel Press, 1953, wood engraving, 220x130mm

10

Figure 8: **Channel Crossing**, 1950, wood engraving, 85x127mm

Figure 9: **Man on the Quay**, 1955, wood engraving, 109x141mm

11

at the bottom of each page the artist alternated humorous subjects with abstract patterns, providing a satisfying balance to the overall design (Pl. 8).

In 1953, Christopher Sandford of the Golden Cockerel Press, who 'admired enormously' Geoffrey Wales' work, commissioned illustrations for *Nelson's Letters from the Leeward Islands*, and once again was obviously pleased with the results, considering the illustrations quite different from anything the Press had had before. He was delighted by 'a nice touch of humour here and there', and enjoyed Geoffrey's use of flags, guns, tridents and anchors (Fig. 7).[4]

The linear element in the designs is often handled quite sketchily. The headpieces are in a predominantly white-line technique with a strong use of the black areas, providing an exciting visual contrast with the circular inner vignette, which animated and complemented the printed page (Pl. 15). A jaunty cockerel in the colophon and the sea-horse on the title-page added to the general appeal of the book.

By comparison, the illustrations for the Folio Society edition of *Drake's Raid on the Treasure Train*, in 1954, appear more conventional, although there is still amazing energy and movement here, particularly where the galleons are portrayed in battles and in storms.

A real stylistic change, however, appeared in Geoffrey Wales' independent wood engravings during the 1950s. Channel Crossing, 1950 (Fig. 8), typifies the decorative compositions of earlier decades. But now his work gradually became less naturalistic. The elements of the design were broken down and reassembled into complicated spatial relationships to form a kaleidoscope of evocative imagery arranged with geometric precision. Great play was made of abstracted, patterned design. In one of the best works from the middle of this period, Man on the Quay, 1955 (Fig. 9), an assemblage of juxtaposed objects and figures is suspended in ambiguous space.

There are stylistic affinities in this image with the work of the neo-romantic artist John Minton during the 1940s; and Jankel Adler's paintings included similar semi-cubist figures, formal structures and surface patterning. Geoffrey Wales had always kept a firm eye on the artistic developments of the avant-garde, and although he appeared to have few close personal connections with the more progressive of British artists, there is no doubt that he was aware of their work, occasionally developing his own art along complementary lines. He was knowledgeable and well-informed about European art, and,

---

[4] Chambers, David and Sandford, Christopher, *Cock-a-Hoop*, Part 4 from the Bibliography of the Golden Cockerel Press, 1949-1961, Private Libraries Association, 1961, p.24.

alongside many other post-war British artists, absorbed the influence of Picasso and Klee whose work was now to be seen at exhibitions and galleries in London.

Other contemporary British influences, possibly Piper and Sutherland, may have led during the late 1950s to a group of works where a more calligraphic and freer use of the engraver's tools is evident. In the strange, insect-like form of Dancer in a Dry Place (Pl.17), the marks could be associated more with the pen than with the graver and refer back to the slightly earlier illustrative work for *Nelson's Letters*. The adaptation of the medium to this more expressionist mode could have been necessitated by the rather strange imaginings which occur in Geoffrey's work at the time. The poignancy of Dancer in a Dry Place and The Prisoner (Pl. 18) may relate to the unease seen in many works of those Cold War years, but may also express feelings of personal isolation and constraint. Certainly, Geoffrey's new appointment as a lecturer at Norwich School of Art in 1953 had not provided an entirely favourable environment and he felt increasing tension at the lack of encouragement he was experiencing for his prints from the contemporary art world and from his colleagues at the art school.

Geoffrey Wales' appointment as Lecturer in Graphic Design at Norwich had resulted in a move for the family to a house in Heigham Grove, near the centre of the city. The Graphic Design Department at this time consisted of around twenty students with just one member of staff. Geoffrey ran his department conscientiously and enjoyed his work, although he disliked the internal politics and power struggles inherent in any institution and tended to avoid much personal interaction with his colleagues. When the Coldstream Report, published in 1960 and enacted through the subsequent years, brought about fundamental re-structuring in the methods of art school teaching and a break with traditional attitudes and approaches to art education,[5] Geoffrey continued to maintain his own methods and work ethic, and became rather isolated as newer staff around him assumed a more relaxed attitude to their teaching. He was a perfectionist and would not accept compromise over correct methods and artistic procedure. However, he was kindly and approachable and impressed his colleagues and his students with his sincerity and artistic integrity. His abler pupils, inspired by his high standards and encouragement,

[5] Allthorpe Guyton, Marjorie, *A Happy Eye, A School of Art in Norwich 1845-1982,* London 1982, p.120ff.

produced their best work under his guidance.

Geoffrey's involvement with current art movements and the wider cultural world was not only as a member of staff in an art school, but also as an active critic of the local and national scene. From 1957 until the mid-1960s, he wrote a regular column in the East Anglian newspaper, the *Eastern Daily Press*, which revealed his understanding of many periods and styles of art as well as his highly developed critical sense. He was equally at home writing on El Greco or Crome as he was on contemporary artists such as Bridget Riley or Henry Moore:

> In almost all of Moore's work there is this concern for discovery, an attempt to find the meaning of experience, and this is the chief reason why he has been able to give British sculpture a vitality and beauty which it has too often lacked in the past. He reminds us that beauty, like truth, has many shades of meaning.
> (*EDP* 1965)

The column covered most of the important visiting exhibitions of national and international art that were mounted at the Castle Museum in Norwich, and also many of the local art shows in the county. To the latter, Geoffrey Wales brought a perceptive eye and a helpful, judgemental approach. He often found the effort involved in writing these pieces, and the demands of meeting a deadline, difficult to cope with, but he always endeavoured to find something encouraging and useful to say.

His critical faculties were exercised in another way at the meetings of the Norwich 20 Group to which he and Marjorie belonged. (Marjorie now had the time to return to her painting and was producing large abstract works which explored colour fields and the movement of light). The Norwich 20 was a lively gathering of practising artists who based themselves on the same idea of self-help, friendly criticism and mutual encouragement that fostered the 19th century Norwich School of painters. The 1960s were a high point of the Group's existence; it counted among its members artists of repute such as Leslie Davenport, Mary Newcomb, Jeffrey Camp and Michael Andrews. Another member was the Reverend Willis Feast, who was the vicar at Booton - a great character, a Bohemian and a poet as well as a painter and engraver; in earlier days he had been the friend and supporter of Wyndham Lewis and he still knew personally many of the avant-garde in both art and literature. Artists of the time, including David Hockney, Lucien Freud and Peter Blake, came to stay at his vast rectory and were invited to attend the meetings of the Group. These lively and vociferous gatherings were held at the Wild Man pub in Norwich,

Figure 10: Collage c. 1960/62, printed papers, colour papers, frottage etc, on card, 145x220mm

Figure 11: Collage c. 1960/62, printed papers, colour papers, frottage etc, on card, 150x265mm

15

Figure 12: Collage c. 1960/62, printed papers, frottage etc, on card, 135x300mm

Figure 13: Collage c. 1960/62, printed papers, colour papers, frottage etc, on card, 152x210mm

16

where, as the members discussed each others' work and art in general, Geoffrey Wales was an active participant, his outspoken and penetrating comments stimulating a vigorous response from his fellow members.

Nearing fifty, his role in this group could have summarised his position thus far: a discriminating observer, conversant with contemporary art and the avant-garde, a teacher of undoubted integrity and intelligence, but, so far, modest in both aspiration and artistic achievement. In the ensuing decades, however, he would bridge that gap, not by embracing current artistic fashions, but by the maturing of his art in line with the tenets of his own generation, which were themselves in the authentic tradition of modernism. The short-term obscurity of this achievement was guaranteed by its being done in wood engraving, which the thrust of contemporary printmaking, as well as the Coldstream reforms, had ruthlessly sidelined.

By the 1960s the evolving style in Geoffrey Wales' wood engravings involved even more fragmented imagery and reduction of form, but it was becoming obvious that the more classical and controlled aspects that had always been present in his prints were gaining ascendancy over the expressionistic gestures and neo-romantic styles with which he had sometimes engaged. During the early 1960s he began to make collages: small, beautifully executed assemblages which were created from his own printed papers, together with sections of frottage. They give the impression of being experimental exercises, exploring form, texture and tone, and to have been developed from the many drawings that filled his sketchbooks. Most could be described as abstract compositions, though they still suggest the landscape and coastal subjects that had inspired them (Figs. 10-13).

Both he and Marjorie displayed collages at an exhibition at the Norwich School of Art Gallery in 1965. According to a contemporary review by Hamilton Wood of the *Eastern Evening News*, these abstract works appeared 'modern without being provocative'. Geoffrey's collages in particular were described as evoking the coastal subjects of their titles with texture and geometry, but, with no recourse to direct representation, they demanded active contemplation from the spectator. After the exhibition, the hundreds of collages Geoffrey had produced over a period of four to five years were relegated to cardboard boxes. Only a few were shown alongside wood engravings in later exhibitions. One can only assume that they had served their purpose, forming an integral part in his resolution of conceptual problems.

Figure 14: Geoffrey Wales drawing on the beach at Happisburg, Norfolk.
(Photograph: the artist's family)

In the wood engravings of this period, due to the precise nature of the medium, the experimentation carried on in drawing and collage reached explicit conclusions. A print made in 1963, Winter Sea (Pl. 21) shows not only the use of familiar marine objects, but a juxtaposition of these simplified but recognisable motifs against a purely formalist interpretation of the sea, created by pattern and texture. Together with a group of still life subjects, which were again reduced to flat patterns and textures, Winter Sea marks Geoffrey Wales' final rejection of more personal and self-revelatory figurative styles and his adoption of a controlled and abstract mode of expression.

He was never entirely happy, though, to call his work abstract. He emphasised that the forms he used were always strongly related to the subject matter from which they had evolved. He wrote,

...the problem of the completely abstract image remains. Here the formal qualities of the work take over at the expense of the subject matter. Speaking for myself, I feel the need for a subject - indeed for me the subject dictates the character of the print. If my work seems at times to be abstract, it is because I am using visual metaphors to express my subject.[6]

The subject matter was still predominantly to do with the features of the British shoreline: the rocks, the pools and the stones, and the sea itself with its everchanging moods, light effects and patterns. His family fondly remember the many hours they all spent on the beach, finding interesting stones and rocks for Geoffrey, who filled sketch book after sketch book with drawings and designs (Fig. 14). He wrote,

The clarity of the light by the sea and the sharply defined, clear cut shapes of marine objects have always suggested ideas for prints. Subject matter of this kind can lend itself to images which owe something to abstraction in that they are abstracted from nature, rather than copied from nature.[7]

The move towards abstraction, far from being the adoption of a current artistic trend, was, for Geoffrey Wales, the culmination of an intellectual process which began with his understanding of modern concepts in art and developed from his ability to examine the essence of his subject and to represent that essence by the refinement of form, line, space and light. The subject of his image was always uppermost in his mind, as his own statements and his copious notes and sketches reveal (Fig. 15). The imagery was not just a formal exercise but resulted

---

[6] *Multiples*, No. 7, 1987, p.66.
[7] *Multiples*, No. 7, 1987, p.66.

19

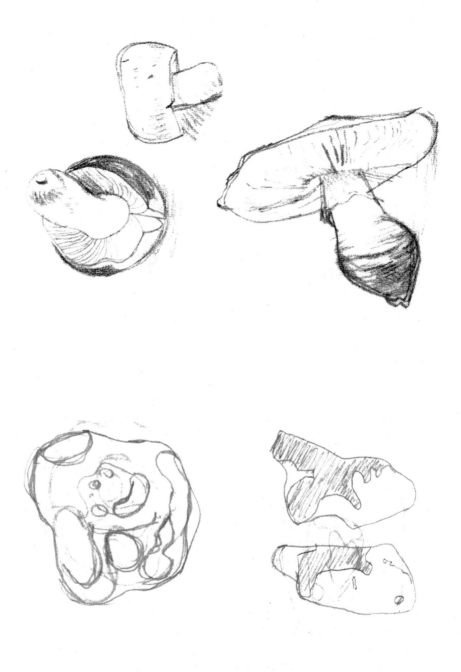

Figure 15: Pencil drawings from sketch books and notebooks, mushrooms
dated 30.7.60 and stones 26.7.80

from the radical simplification of natural appearances; these visual ideas were most positively and deliberately 'abstracted from nature'.

It is probably useful at this point to consider Geoffrey Wales' prints in the wider context of abstract printmaking in Britain. Abstract images were certainly much in evidence during the 1950s and 60s, and in many ways Geoffrey Wales' work complemented the contemporary landscape painting and printmaking of the St. Ives artists such as Peter Lanyon, William Scott and those others who shared the same interest in the dialogue between abstraction and landscape or nature. But, historically, abstract images in wood engraving have been unusual. Edward Wadsworth produced some non-figurative woodcuts during his Vorticist period before 1920, but the first purely abstract compositions in wood engraving had appeared in the work of Paul Nash. The illustrations he engraved for *Genesis* (1923-4) were non-representational and purely formal, using hard, geometric shapes as well as poetic arabesques. Later, Nash used a more concrete abstraction in his illustrations for *A Song about Tzar Ivan Vasilyevitch*, where the forms were even more geometric. But this period of abstract imagery was short-lived, and by the 1930s Nash had revealed his antipathy to forms which did not 'visually acknowledge the organic and natural world'.[8]

In the 1930s, Ben Nicholson executed a single abstract woodcut (one of the most interesting prints of the period), and a few other wood engravers were prepared to extend their work into the area of abstraction. From 1935-38 Blair Hughes-Stanton produced a series of independent wood engravings which experimented with abstract art in a technically flawless but rather lifeless way; and John Tandy had engraved clear, bold abstract prints from as early as 1928, which received much critical acclaim and attention. John Buckland Wright had been stimulated into producing several non-representational wood engravings during the 1930s by his association with Atelier 17 in Paris, run by Stanley Hayter; although most of these works were ultimately based on the human form, wood engravings such as his Composition no.6 (1935) display a perfect command of abstract rhythms.

During the same period, Gertrude Hermes and John Farleigh produced semi-abstract compositions, but their work always made reference to the organic and the figurative and never underwent a

---

[8] Eates, Margot, *Paul Nash, 1889-1946*, London 1973, pp.47-48.

complete adoption of abstract form.

By the 1940s, the demise of wood engraving was to obscure the work of many interesting but lesser known artists who continued to work in the medium. However, few of these wood engravers engaged with contemporary movements in art, and the technique showed little sign of adapting itself to the post-war vision. By the 1950s, wood engraving was rarely used except for book illustration and it had become the Cinderella of the printmaking media. Sadly, only a few artists had emerged who were still prepared to exploit the artistic potentialities of the wood block in independent prints, and their work was denied a wider audience by the lack of commercial interest and exhibiting facilities.

One of the few other artists to make abstract wood engravings in the post-war years, apart from Geoffrey Wales, was Albert Garrett. Garrett became President of the Society of Wood Engravers in 1967 and wrote extensively on wood engraving and wood engravers. His own prints were rhythmic and thematic, often displaying his fascination with the effects of light and illustrating his theories in relation to printmaking. In spite of exhibiting his prints regularly at the Society of Wood Engravers and with the Royal Society of Painter-Etchers and Engravers, his work was mostly overlooked and not appreciated. He was in a similar position to that of Geoffrey Wales, belonging neither to the avant-garde in printmaking at that time, who

Figure 16: **The Waves**, 1969/70, wood engraving, 103x160mm

tended to use the larger and colourful printmaking techniques such as linocut and lithography, nor to the smaller, safer world of illustration and conventional representation.

Geoffrey Wales was therefore one of the few artists of the twentieth century to explore the potential of wood engraving for non-figurative ends, in recognising its suitability for his own particular kind of reductive abstract imagery. His cerebral and committed response to some of the concepts of abstract art did not require large, colourful statements; the restrictions and limitations of the wood block enhanced the slow and deliberate evolution of the forms he sought to extract from the organic and natural world.

The wood engravings produced during the late 1960s and the 1970s (Pls. 22-39) represent the culmination of this abstract genre: taut, aniconic images executed with strength and vigour. The blocks are deeply cut. A web of fine lines is often set against larger areas of black, for visual impact. The quality of inking and printing enhances this juxtaposition and adds to the coruscating dance of such images as Flowering Ocean (Pl. 25) and The Waves (Fig. 16). He was also

Figure17: **Rocks and Reed Bed**, 1978, wood engraving, 137x75mm

23

experimenting with the use of separate blocks to form a diptych or a triptych; an example being Waterfront Gear (Pl. 22), where the compositional bursts serve to separate the elements contained within the image, extending them across a wider front and through several focal points.

Throughout all the prints, the themes of the coast, the waves, rocks, sea and shore, continued to be worked through with an intense scrutiny. In the series of prints he entitled White Rock I -V (Pls. 30-34), which evolved over a period of three years, he returned time and time again to the theme, extending, reworking and refining the idea and its implications. Each print brings a different nuance of meaning to the simple motif of the rocks that lay in and beneath the water. The appearance of each rock - its shape, its shadows, its various facets and gem-like qualities as the sun and sea play over it - is reduced to brilliant black and white. The prints exploit the potential of the wood block for its textural properties (by the use of a variety of engraved marks), and for expressing dimensional complexity, as seen in the overlapping planes of White Rock V (Pl. 34).

Though in the late 1970s and the 1980s titles for his prints such as Quiet Water, Stones by the Sea and Baroque Shell indicated that coastal and aquatic motifs still held their fascination for him, other prints of the period, Dry Walls (Pl. 36) and Quay with Buoys (Pl. 39) re-introduced elements from earlier prints and mark a flow and a cross-fertilisation with previous motifs, now mastered and refined. Although every one of Geoffrey Wales' abstract prints is a distinct and individual response to a motif, they share a vocabulary of marks which allows the viewer to understand the language of what he called his visual metaphors. This is seen very clearly in a print of the late 1970s, Rocks and Reed Bed (Fig. 17) where the vertical lines are not only one of the formal aspects of the composition, but are marks which act as signifiers for the organic verticality of the reeds suggested by the title.

With a little concentration, it is always possible for the viewer to be drawn into the small, perfect model of the world that Geoffrey Wales created in his wood engravings.

Over the years, Geoffrey's production of wood engravings became an even more private activity, the prints that resulted being limited to just one or two impressions from the block. Unless they were destined to be shown at the Royal Society of Painter-Etchers and Engravers' annual show or at the now sporadic exhibitions of the Society of Wood Engravers, they were given away to friends or simply stored in a folder. Two shows, at the Pottergate Gallery in Norwich in 1974 and at the Norwich School of Art Gallery in 1978, interrupted this flow of unrecognised endeavour. In many ways Geoffrey Wales' attitude can be compared with that of an earlier artist and printmaker whose work he admired greatly, the Italian Giorgio Morandi (1890-1964). Although Morandi was to achieve international recognition for his art, he was also a teacher who worked in self-imposed exile, privately exploring the artistic possibilities of the same, repeated subject-matter. Geoffrey Wales' abstract wood engravings exhibit the classic severity and sound craftsmanship that are apparent in Morandi's etchings of simple bottles and jugs.[9]

Geoffrey continued to produce wood engravings until 1985 when, at the age of 73, failing health and deteriorating eyesight began severely to restrict his work. The last blocks were cut with little vigour. Only a few were ever proofed. The prints and the blocks were carefully stored away with the many others which constituted his lifetime's work. He died on 25th April 1990.

In spite of his lack of interest - indeed antipathy to - any form of self-promotion, Geoffrey Wales' work always attracted serious critical attention. He is listed in all the major dictionaries of printmakers and his prints are discussed in the books and articles written on British wood engraving since the 1950s by Thomas Balston ,[10] John Buckland Wright,[11] Albert Garrett[12] and, recently, James Hamilton.[13] In the early 1990s the Castle Museum in Norwich acquired a representative sample of his prints, and the Ashmolean Museum in Oxford added a large, comprehensive selection to its extensive collection of 20th century British wood engraving.

By those who knew him, Geoffrey Wales is remembered as an inspiring teacher and a modest, generous and intelligent man. As a wood engraver, he is acknowledged as an important and accomplished practitioner who explored and extended the conceptual and pictorial boundaries of the medium. But beyond that, the fifty or so engravings of his late period of work serve to refute everything that was implied at the time and has been said since about the limitations of wood engraving as such: Geoffrey Wales used the most essential features of the medium in work which lies in the very mainstream of the artistic concerns of the century.

---

[9] For Morandi's Etchings see *L'Opera Grafica: Rispondenze e Variezioni*, Ed. M. Cordaro, Ex Catalogue, Rome, Institute Nazionale per la Grafica, Dec. 1990 - Feb. 1991.

[10] Balston, Thomas, *English Wood Engravers 1900-1950*, London 1951.

[11] Buckland Wright, John, *Etching and Engraving*, London 1953.

[12] Garrett, Albert, *British Wood Engravers of the 20th Century*, 1980.

[13] Hamilton, James, *Wood Engraving and the Woodcut in Britain, c. 1890-1990*, London 1994.

THE WOOD ENGRAVINGS

Plate 1
a. **Pier End**, c.1935, 50x50mm
b. **Roof and Jetty**, c.1935, 50x50mm
c. Headpiece to *The Pilgrim Fathers*, Golden
   Cockerel Press, 1939, 65x105mm

a

b

c

Plate 2
Yellow Tower, 1939, 102x154mm (reduced to 75%)

30

31

Plate 3
a. **Sharp Attack**, 1944, 72x102mm
b. **Northern Waters**, 1942, 75x100mm

a

b

33

Plate 4
Lot 34, 1947, 72x100mm

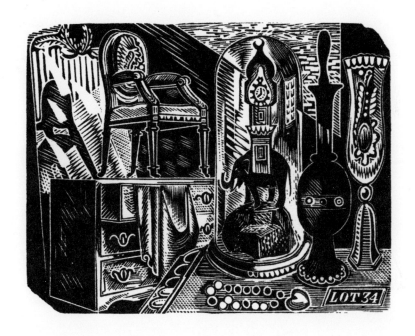

Plate 5
Gothic Garden, 1948, 177x128mm (reduced to 75%)

36

37

Plate 6
The Moonflower, 1948, 175x125mm (reducedto 75%)

Plate 7
a. **March**, 1950, 90x126mm (reduced to 90%)
b. **Harbour**, 1949, 100x125mm (reduced to 90%)

a

b

41

Plate 8
a. *Kynoch Diary*, 1950, Illustration for May. 103x70mm
b & c. *Kynoch Diary*, 1950, Page motifs. 25x50mm

a

b

c

Plate 9
View from a Window, 1950, 126x100mm

Plate 10
Rendezvous, 1950, 180x128mm (reduced to 75%)

46

Plate 11
Springtide, 1951, 180x197mm (reduced to 50%)

Plate 12
The Clock, 1950, 177x188mm (reduced to 50%)

Plate 13
Bright Morning, 1950, 156x186mm (reduced to 50%)

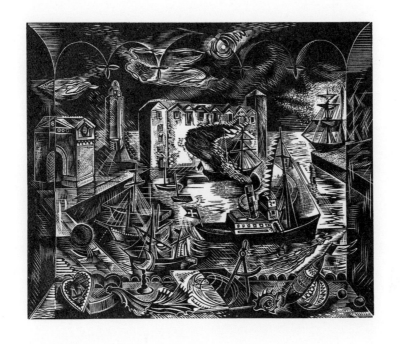

Plate 14
Gothic Landscape, 1951, 179x230mm (reduced to 50%)

Plate 15
a. *Nelson's Letters from the Leeward Islands.* Golden
   Cockerel Press, 1953, Headpiece, 65x130mm
b. *Nelson's Letters*, Colophon, 82x50mm
c. *Nelson's Letters*, Title Page, 57x57mm

a

b

c

Plate 16
South Coast, 1954, 129x93mm

Plate 17
Dancer in a Dry Place, 1957, 174x147mm (reduced to 75%)

61

Plate 18
The Prisoner, 1957, 155x184mm (reduced to 75%)

Plate 19
April Sun, 1960, 179x152mm (reduced to 75%)

Plate 20
Landscape and Objects, 1962, 99x122mm

Plate 21
Winter Sea, 1963, 134x152mm (reduced to 75%)

68

Plate 22
Waterfront Gear, 1965, 126x232mm (reduced to 50%)

70

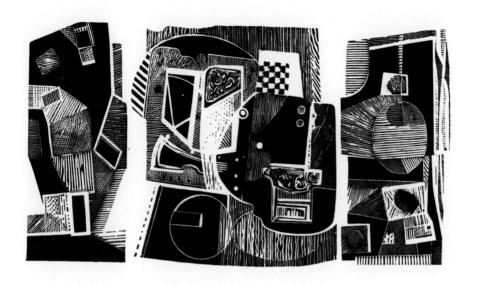

Plate 23
Wooden Wall, 1966, 125x199mm (reduced to 50%)

72

Plate 24
Crystalline Vegetable, 1967/8, 65x150mm

Plate 25
Flowering Ocean, 1969/70, 204x205 (reduced to 50%)

Plate 26
Glass Net, 1967/68, 125x200mm (reduced to 50%)

Plate 27
Shells and Rockform, 1969/70, 123x120mm (reduced to 75%)

80

Plate 28
Moving Forms, 1969/70, 100x145mm (reduced to 75%)

83

Plate 29
October Landscape, 1970/71, 113x114mm

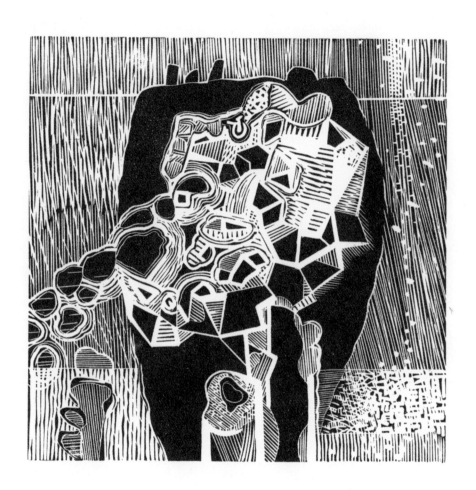

Plate 30
White Rock I, 1971/2, 129x128mm

86

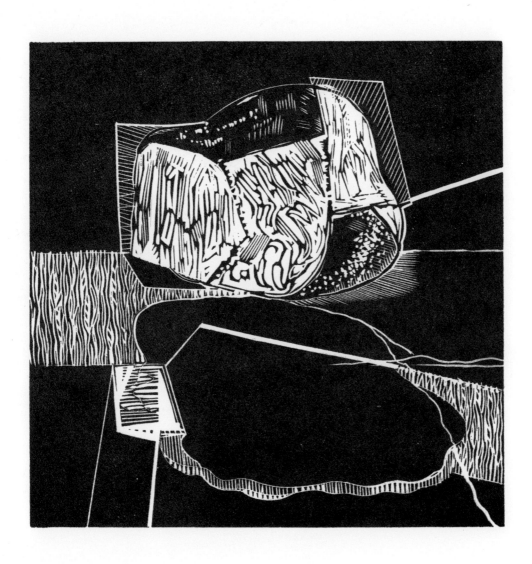

Plate 31
White Rock II, 1971/2, 127x128mm

Plate 32
White Rock III, 1971/2, 127x128mm

90

91

Plate 33
White Rock IV, 1973/4, 129x130mm

92

93

Plate 34
White Rock V, 1973/4, 127x130mm

94

Plate 35
Shadow and Water, 1972/3, 149x79mm

97

Plate 36
Dry Walls, 1976/7, 117x73mm

98

Plate 37
Paper Flowers, 1976/7, 97x87mm

100

Plate 38
Beach and Sea Wall, 1978, 115x115mm

Plate 39
Quay with Buoys, 1979, 102x73mm

Plate 40
Stones by the Sea, 1980, 125x104mm

107

Plate 41
Potshards, 1980, 126x102mm

109

Plate 42
Sea Wall, 1983, 115x115mm

110

111

Plate 43
Nordic Stone, 1983, 142x75mm

112

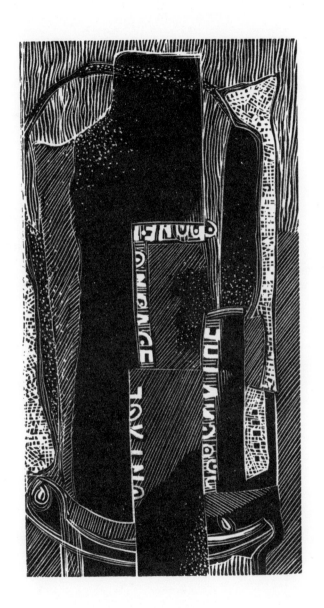

113

Plate 44
The Game, 1984, 90x115

Plate 45
Baroque Shell, 1985, 127x102mm

CHRONOLOGY

1912   Born, 26th May, Margate, Kent.

1929-33   Studied at Thanet School of Art.

1932   Won competition to design playing card for de la Rue.

1933-37   Studied at Royal College of Art.

1936   Assisted Barnet Freedman with mural decorations for the Strand Underpass for the Coronation of George VI and Queen Elizabeth.

1937   Assisted John Nash with mural decorations for the British Pavilion at the Paris Exhibition.

1937   Studied at the Central School of Arts and Crafts.

1937-40   Taught in Canterbury Group of Art Schools.

1940   Married the painter Marjorie Skeeles.

1940-46   Flight Lieutenant with the Royal Air Force.

1946   Returned to teaching at Canterbury and living at Lyminge, Kent.

1946   Elected member of the Society of Wood Engravers.

1953   Appointed lecturer at Norwich School of Art.
Moved to 15 Heigham Grove, Norwich.
Prints acquired by Circulation Department of Victoria and Albert Museum to be toured around schools and colleges in an exhibition of British Contemporary Prints.

1957-65   Contributed column as art critic to the Eastern Daily Press.

1957   September: Exhibited with Xylon International in an exhibition at Portoguaro, Italy.

1960   Member of Norwich 20 Group.

1961   Elected Fellow of the Royal Society of Painter-Etchers and Engravers.

1965   Joint exhibition of collages with Marjorie at Norwich School of Art Gallery.

1967   20 May - 11 June: Work included in an Exhibition of East Anglian prints at Gainsborough's House, Sudbury, Suffolk.

1974   November: Exhibition at the Pottergate Gallery, Norwich, Prints and Collages.

1977   Retired from teaching.

1978   Exhibition at Norwich School of Art Gallery, Prints and Collages.

1990   Died, Norwich, April 25th.

1991   Retrospective Exhibition, Wood Engraving and Collages by Geoffrey Wales R.E. at the 20th Century Gallery, London.

CHECKLIST OF BOOKS ILLUSTRATED

1939

THE PILGRIM FATHERS:
A JOURNAL OF THEIR COMING IN THE MAYFLOWER TO NEW
ENGLAND AND THEIR LIFE AND ADVENTURES THERE.

Edited with a preface and notes by Theodore Besterman.
Eight engravings by Geoffrey Wales.

Published by the Golden Cockerel Press

300 copies

Frontispiece
Title page
Six illustrations

1950

THE KYNOCH PRESS DIARY FOR 1950.

Wood engravings by Geoffrey Wales.

Published by The Kynoch Press

Title page
Illustrations for each month
Motifs for each page

1953

NELSON'S LETTERS FROM THE LEEWARD ISLANDS
AND OTHER ORIGINAL DOCUMENTS IN THE PUBLIC RECORD OFFICE
AND THE BRITISH MUSEUM.

Edited by Geoffrey Rawson with notes by Professor Michael Lewis
and engravings by Geoffrey Wales.

Published by the Golden Cockerel Press.

300 numbered copies, 1-60 specially bound.

Frontispiece
Title page
Seven illustrations
Colophon

1954

SIR FRANCIS DRAKE'S RAID ON THE TREASURE TRAINS: BEING THE
MEMORABLE RELATION OF HIS VOYAGE TO THE WEST INDIES IN 1572.

Edited by Janet and John Hampden with wood engravings by Geoffrey Wales.

Published by the Folio Society.

Frontispiece
Seven illustrations

CHECKLIST OF WOOD ENGRAVINGS

This list has been compiled from the edition books kept by Geoffrey Wales from 1935. Nearly all the prints are on high quality Japan paper. Size is given in millimetres, height before width.

Before 1936

Pier End	not editioned	50x50
Buoy in Sea	not editioned	50x50
Roof and Jetty	not editioned	50x50
Sea through Ruined Arch	not editioned	50x50

1936

Boat and Jetty	not editioned	32x127
House on Windswept Hill	not editioned	127x103
Swan on Pond	not editioned	101x102
Fishing Boats	not editioned	170x110
The Waterfall	not editioned	50x125

1938

Sun and Rain	edition of 50	75x100

1939

Mont St. Vincent	edition of 50	108x100
Man in an Aeroplane (4 colour blocks)	not editioned	84x124
Ophelia (colour blocks)	edition of 50	102x154

Quayside with Church and Boats (printed in blue)	not editioned	40x82
Yellow Tower (also printed with 2 colour blocks)	edition of 50	102x154

1942

Northern Waters	edition of 50	75x100

1944

Sharp Attack	not editioned	72x102

1947

Lot 34	edition of 25	72x100
In a Glass Darkly (also printed with 3 colour blocks)	edition of 50	152x80
The Letter	edition of 50	70x102
The Inquisition	edition of 25	118x86
Strange Head	not editioned	123x90
Psalm 148	edition of 50	150x135

1948

Midwinter Night	edition of 25	175x120
Spring Morning	edition of 25	172x124
High Summer	edition of 25	not traced
Flower Maiden	edition of 50	177x123
Gothic Garden	edition of 50	177x128
Autumn	edition of 25	177x128
The Moonflower	edition of 25	175x125
Dressmakers Dummy	not editioned	93x82

1949

Harbour (printed also in yellow and blue; design for Harpers Bazaar)	not editioned	100x125
The Rock Pool	edition of 25	140x75

1950

Bright Morning	edition of 25	156x186
March	edition of 50	90x126
Sun and Rain	edition of 50	70x182
Fordwich	not editioned	90x108
Shuttlesfield	not editioned	129x115
Channel Crossing	edition of 50	85x127
A Suggestion for February	not editioned	103x72
A Suggestion for October	not editioned	103x72
Quiet Afternoon	edition of 25	154x185
The Clock	edition of 25	177x188
The Ladder of Gold	edition of 25	1st st. 150x180 2nd st.114x133
Silver Arrow	edition of 25	90x116
Rendezvous	edition of 25	180x128
Prospect	edition of 25	157x100
Landscape (also with 2 colour blocks)	not editioned	70x125
After Rain (also with yellow block)	not editioned	137x77
View from Window	not editioned	1st st. 152x110 2nd st.126x100

Still Life	not editioned	75x100

1951

City Life (Jazz City) (also with colour block)	edition of 25	165x99
The Bay	edition of 25	160x179
Springtide	edition of 50	180x197
Wisden (illustration for Wisden)	not editioned	115x82
Iron Gate	edition of 50	116x141
The Window	edition of 25	179x230
Gothic Landscape	edition of 25	179x230

1954

Embarkation for the Indies	edition of 25	225x175
House of Cards	not editioned	115x84
South Coast	edition of 25	129x93
Signal Point	edition of 25	102x146

1955

February Landscape	edition of 25	89x141
Man on the Quay	edition of 25	109x141
The Jugglers	not editioned	97x95
The Magic Cup	edition of 25	125x90
The Light and Darkness	edition of 25	75x137

1956

Two Puppets	edition of 25	128x95

War Lord	edition of 25	224x120
Sea King	edition of 25	203x126
The Sad Clown	edition of 25	125x64
The Giants	not editioned	127x102

1957

Aquarium	edition of 25	153x180
Dancer in a Dry Place	edition of 25	175x147
The Prisoner	edition of 25	155x184

1960

The Estuary	edition of 25	177x286
April Sun	edition of 25	179x152

1961

Fungi	edition of 25	126x184
Pebbles and Water	edition of 25	91x124
Stones on Beach (woodcut)	edition of 25	270x550

1962

Cottage Window	edition of 25	79x141
Objects in a Window	edition of 25	116x162
Landscape and Objects	edition of 25	99x122
Sea Wall (woodcut)	edition of 25	280x490

1963

Machine in Fields	edition of 25	not traced

Winter Sea	edition of 25	134x152
Water Edge	edition of 25	112x125
Promenade	edition of 25	not traced, blocks destroyed
Found Object	edition of 25	not traced

1964

Falling Forms	edition of 25	129x128
Rising Forms	edition of 25	128x129

1965

Waterfront Gear (1967: end blocks printed separately)	edition of 25	126x232

1966

Wooden Wall	edition of 25	125x199

1967/68

Crystalline Vegetable	edition of 25	65x150
Water Garden	edition of 25	167x280
Sea Drift	edition of 25	132x177
Glass Net	edition of 25	125x200
Marine Machine 2 (also on larger sheet with colour block)	edition of 25	162x105
Underwater Forms	edition of 25	not traced, block destroyed
Objects and Water	edition of 25	not traced
In and Out	edition of 25	not traced

1969/70

Black Motive (woodcut)	edition of 25	330x290
Flowering Ocean	edition of 25	204x205
The Waves	edition of 25	103x160
Dark Channel (River Channel)	edition of 25	160x216
Moving Forms	edition of 25	100x145
Forms at Rest	edition of 25	100x145
Shells and Rockform	edition of 25	123x120
Wave Breaking (woodcut)	edition of 25	237x450
Summertime	edition of 25	100x78
Midwinter	edition of 25	115x90

1970/71

October Landscape	edition of 25	113x114
November Landscape	edition of 25	113x113

1971/72

White Rock I	edition of 25	129x128
White Rock II	edition of 25	127x128
White Rock III	edition of 25	127x128
Winter Wood	edition of 25	100x75

1972/73

Light over Water	edition of 25	110x88
Shadow and Water	edition of 25	149x79 Recut 112x79

1973/74

Coastal Image	edition of 25	not traced
White Rock IV	edition of 25	129x130
White Rock V	edition of 25	127x130

1975

Landscape with Rocks	edition of 25	160x103
Shell Garden	edition of 25	140x90
Water Garden	edition of 25	130x107
Garden in Winter	edition of 25	140x88

1976

Black Boulder	edition of 25	86x139
Glass Fruit I	edition of 25	87x105
Glass Fruit II	edition of 25	70x102

1976/77

Dry Walls	edition of 25	117x73
Paper Flowers	edition of 25	97x87

1978

Beach and Sea Wall	edition of 25	115x115
Garden Cluster	edition of 25	140x90
Rocks and Reed Bed	edition of 25	137x75

1979

Quay with Buoys	edition of 25	102x73
Hill Stream	edition of 25	75x97

1980

Quiet Water	edition of 25	94 diam.
Stones by the Sea	edition of 25	125x104
Potshards	edition of 25	126x102

1983

Sea Wall	edition of 25	115x115
Rock Rose	edition of 25 two states	115x115
Nordic Stone	edition of 25	142x75

1984

Three Flint Stones	edition of 25	115x115
The Game	edition of 25	90x115

1985

Cold Sea Wreck (Shadow and Water recut)	edition of 25	90x142
Baroque Shell	edition of 25	127x102

After 1985

Water Plants	not editioned	80x78
Firethorn	not editioned	102x80
Wood and Stone	not editioned	140x77